Romantic Portrait of a Natural Disaster

poems by

Hannah Cajandig-Taylor

Finishing Line Press
Georgetown, Kentucky

Romantic Portrait of a Natural Disaster

For Lori Jobe, my kindred spirit.

ACKNOWLEDGMENTS

"Self Destruction & other disasters to think about" first appeared in *Coffin Bell Journal*
"You as Apocalypse" first appeared in *Gordon Square Review*
"Daydrinking on The River Styx" first appeared in *Gravitas*
"Cliff Jumping at St. Mary's Glacier" & "You as Stormchaser" first appeared in *LandLocked Magazine*
"Planetary Geology" first appeared in *Pittsburgh Poetry Journal*
"Relativity Theory" first appeared in *Pretty Owl Poetry*
"Moonstruck" & "Anaphylactic Shock" first appeared in *Rising Phoenix Review*
"Lovely" first appeared in *Snapdragon: A Journal of Art & Healing*
"Self Portrait as Star Burning Out" first appeared in *The Sonora Review*

To all of the places that have given a lovely home to my work— I can never
express my gratitude enough. Thank you for hearing me, & for continuing to
make the literary world a beautiful place to be.

Publisher: Leah Maines
Editor: Christen Kincaid
Cover Art: Daisy Crane
Author Photo: Heath Cajandig
Cover Design: Elizabeth Maines McCleavy

Order online: www.finishinglinepress.com
also available on amazon.com

Author inquiries and mail orders:
Finishing Line Press
P. O. Box 1626
Georgetown, Kentucky 40324
U. S. A.

Table of Contents

"We are created by being destroyed"

—Franz Wright

i.

Baptizing The Planet as an Act of God

The internet once told me to always ask for another drink, just in case
the supervolcano in Yellowstone decides to explode & bury us
in coughed-up ash, when there are still countless things
to put in the time capsule, still endless versions of *ars poetica* to wear out.
      Here's to a future of biodegradable cars with gas tanks full

of floating algae, to some plastic tomorrow where I am done searching
for what causes a winter sky to turn orange. Spoiler alert: it was a wildfire
in California, scorching the last member of a species before some scientist
could dig it up, or give it a Christian name. We were made
for the process of unearthing. Do you ever get nostalgic?
Me either. If I lit a match with my breath, maybe I would be

the one to burst aflame, soak my clothes
until their colors become artificial.
      Here's to the broke & broken years,
where some would describe relapse as *an act
of god*, or some divine intervention we consider
necessary, even though we'll all be dead before the last cut
airs on TV. I don't want to think
      about how the world is ending
      about how many hurricanes are constantly forming
      about how pointless it is to be daydreaming in a laundromat
      about how much closer I am standing to the ocean's floor
when I am only a disaster away from it. When earth has finished
another spin cycle & we are no longer rotated
on rinse & repeat, it is true that we will unravel
for the last & first time.

Here's to staining a fence in the rain
& praying at the altar of nobody, palms full of nothing
but splinters, & maybe that's what I get for running
my hands over the surface, for getting wine drunk
at the celebration of life

before death, for desperately wanting any part
of this rotten body to promise
we will not be forgotten.

Anaphylactic Shock

All these fragments from a sting—shrinking & expanding
concurrently, the lower half of a hollow body left behind

like an oblong pill swallowed at eighteen, when I realized
rooms could not be spun by their handles. The numbing will fade

if you want it to, so write about velvet & lacquer,
linoleum & sandpaper—things I can touch

      because I want to feel
like my chest cavity is not out of reach.

Who needs eggshells when there are stingers
thorning their way into my bare feet, as I become

what I did not want to be at all—half heart,
the other part organic machine. Tell me

when you dreamed about radiance, eyes stumbling
over the aurora borealis & its gentle implosion

of the night horizon. For that moment of singularity,
we pretended the wild never bit us

back—as if the plague had been distended
& I had always been willing to survive.

Cliff Jumping at St. Mary's Glacier

This did not happen
when I was standing at the basin

picking rocks from the water
until my heavy hands went numb

       & I was in love with things
created from seismic activity.

I filled my pockets with the fallen
pieces of earth, gesturing in jarring pieces

to everything that treads over it.
If I took a walk one night

on another planet, I would hope
for an overlap in our skies

where the distant stars
would burn cold & weighted

but we would still be able to see
one another from our own

awayness. Even after the moons
       had shifted places

       & the earth's plates
were licked clean of their crumbs,

       I would still be able to miss you.

Watercolored Landscape, Northern Michigan USA

What if it is raining & you are
the only one who can feel

your skin beaded & soaked,
each flinch of hesitation

making its way from the cave
of your chest to the slick

of your knees kissing
the bathroom floor, the wet

of your cheek. I am trying

to make a diagram of you
in a foggy mirror, but cannot

remember how
to shape the vortex

behind your eyes, greener
on the other side

from gazing at the rain
outside, where you become

nothing at all. Nothing
but chill & gaps

screen windows & shutter speed
rainbows down highway 41. No more

stormchasing. No reason to go
down with the sun. Please do not

waste yourself
anywhere but here.

Anxious Astronomy

I'm going to sing to Polaris, the north star, the hotel bar that stole its name, to the dreamscapes outside my window, to the fog-laden lust dripping down its pane, to a singular sentence morphing into bedtime story, you're my misery, my fucked-up starlight, & I mean it when I count the eyelashes drifting from your cheek, when I take your wishes & use my breath, blowing them into the wind with good intentions, have you caught the moon in your right hand, folded it into a bird, released it, watched it float up to the sky, freckled your cheeks with dark stars, & sometimes, evenings like these are floating in a delicate spiral along the tops, serving cocktails to tiredly handsome investors, lawyers in wrinkled ties, pink-heeled women & countless out-of-state businesspeople & pairs of lifelong friends with names like Margaret & Ethel & regulars that stop by often enough to know when an employee is new, & when it's finally over, I end up going home to get high & write weird & sad stories about a weatherman & obsess over cloud formations while listening to The Clash, then more meteorology-based songs like hurricane / hurricanes / always hurricanes / before screaming purple into my skull, wanting to know the answers to hollow questions, like, does your brain ever get the best of you, or do you ever linger between the sun & earth & how do you breath when the universe stops singing back to you.

Ars Poetica as Recited by a Dead Viper
—After Judy Grahn

Maybe spitting venom is just blowing
smoke. Maybe I only breathe in
to push out what is left. Fill me

with green or anything
that makes my hair grow. Fill me
    with brass-colored tulips

      & button black roses,
    the brightest bedroom
yellow chrysanthemums. Pull me closer

or further, love me with my snake eyes
batting as I shed my skin
to leave behind nothing but hollow,

finally something
spellbinding & probably
    a sin, too.

I Pretend My Window is a Spaceship

—After Roger Chaffee, Ed White & Gus Grissom,
late crew of the Apollo 1

to get away, climb eyes-first through
the rectangular window above my bed
catapulting myself at the stars
burning in the distance. I start unfolding

the blinds each night, thought I could
get lucky & let a UFO abduct me
in some galactic getaway car
ripping across the fabric

of the universe. When a world dies,
nobody is around to hear it. Mothers cry
as their sons explode with fire
from inside a rocket, the cause of death

labeled as *an accident*
related to the exploration of space.
Too many times, I am a failure
to launch, unable to save the passengers

clinging to my sinking body. I have heard
the night is shorter on the other side
of the cosmos, but why would I believe
it—this window has never taken me

to any place with light.

Situations

One would think that broken zippers
& unspooled cuckoo clocks
might fit the category, or lipstick pink
doll dresses with torn pockets,
or waking up a half hour too late
      for my great grandfather's funeral.

I am fleeting with nightmares, my brain
spun out of funnel clouds. Storms are
circumstantial, beauty is situational
& I am   still distracted
      by a sinkhole eating Detroit.

In Pennsylvania, a town has been
spouting hellfire for years. Every day
is the end of the world, each season
      braiding a noose
from the daffodil yellow roots
      below my clouded window.

Don't let it rot you—this notion
of fixing & unfixing
& calling it closure. Don't
keep track of the days
      & deaths & paper clocks.

Call this something else. Call this
anything but desirable.
Call this being in love
with any situation
      on the brink of collapse.

Self Portrait as A Meteorologist

The leaves are burning
to supernova. It is the grey

of fall & I am rinsing
my hair down the drain,

humming along to the sky
ripping its own seams

to spill pillow stuffing
& hot air balloons.

My car stands in the flood
of your backyard, lights off

so I can listen to my moonlight
pouring through the crack

in my window. I am wanting
someone to see me

in the front seat, horizon
patterned with floating baskets

while everyone waves down
with their right hand. It ends

with me, driving in silence
until gravity turns against itself.

My dead cells refuse to fly. We wash
yesterday's dirt down the sink, refuse

to fold into a basket. It ends too far
ahead, too soon—in a firestorm

on the Channel Five greenscreen
or some other future   I will never know.

Twenty-Two Degree Halo

We write a letter to the sky & address it to both sides of the sun.

A smudge of light   alone is not enough
for us. I dress in a halo   warn you before the winter storm
dial my frequency to put out   red & sticky blues. You change
the channel. We are nothing   more than scattered
         particles reflecting light
as it passes through us. We bend   see the color with our own eyes
break ourselves open   spill
our painted stomachs. In short   we are basically fucked-up
factories dumping rainbows over everyone in sight—
         giving the command of consumption,
the command of   elongate your spine
         but don't forget to undo it
in a momentary lapse of light like dreaming in static
only existing in the moment   between licking a socket
& feeling it shock your tongue   become numb
         become empty   become
skeletons stretching their bony hands   at the fingers
         of a willow tree   because I too reach
for who I used to be. I dream in piano keys
& yellow umbrellas   an expert at grasping
         for anything that can feel the sun   or breathe
even though I left   part of myself behind   a long time ago.

Planetary Geology

      another cosmic joke— pretending to not be wicked
& servant to Andromeda, dressed in gloom

& reaching for a concrete galaxy
            just a few worlds away. We were
            tectonic—always shifting to become another
            rumble & name the sound of our core

            imploding on itself. I only cling to silent
voices & maybe you'll find me if you crawl

to the center of the earth, cradled in fossils
            & waist-length hair. You'll name the dark
            matter so I won't waste time talking about
            how divine it was to watch a goddess falter

            into a constellation, all golden & sprawling.
She'll smoked your last cigarette

& crush every star you were once
            proud of, each broken bulb of light fractured
            towards us, where we sleep in the backyard
            & wait for the sun to finally burn out.

Lovely

I was a tempest pressed from tea leaves
      & ragdoll wrists bleeding

            into a towel, your books
      muddled with cigarette dreams

& my bones were the porch swing.
      I brushed my teeth to taste iron

            but could only swallow ghosts
      & you, reeking of cinnamon mouthwash

spun me in circles   &   circles
      your carousel horse breathing

& breaking. My haunted bones,
      whiskey drunk & creaking

with your rocking chair, counting the turns
      until I choked & became

            the skeleton girl unraveling
      into blue cotton on the sidewalk.

Even when I am dressed in noise,
      I cannot drown out the quiet

            of everyone else's bad dreams.
      I cannot stop trying to spin silk

from these bones & I have been told
      there is a relationship between art

            & science but I know this feeling
      was carved from ultraviolet

because my damage will not show up
      until later, when I am trying on

          different versions of myself
     & tiptoeing on the hardwood

so as to not bleed onto everything
      I have ever found beautiful.

ii.

Self-Portrait as Star Burning Out

Endings always start the same way—stellar
      nurseries clouded with beginnings

in the form of hydrogen, newborn specks
      bright, birthed in the recesses of nowhere.

They stumble & flash with laughter. For a moment
      you almost feel like a part of something

until suddenly, you are behind glass—you want to choose
      the color of your aura. You choose to be all of them

because you are afraid of grey. Want to be painted
      by any color looking for its chemical match & you are

stroking your bangs, pulsing with questions
      while you are busy deconstructing

drywall & whispering the night away
      beside someone in this carnival

of catastrophes, of montaging through cycles
      of red giants dying into planetary nebulae

down to the smallest prick of light
      until suddenly, darkness—explode & repeat.

Moonstruck

My favorite type of wind loves to pass
between chimes.   She is obsessed with awayness
          & sees stars on the window panes at dawn,
     when my (search) history is coming back

with no results & nothing whole pours out of me.
     She has taken to writing about the haunted
                    woman who was tricked by a ghost
          swallowing glass,   her inside being broken

                    by pieces of broken, & the moon cracks
          a grin   nobody pays attention to. She is crumbling
     in the dusk & again   I have forgotten
the magic word   for *an insincere smile,*

or what to call a linchpin   slipping
          its crater. We chant at the sky
                    & our bare skin chases
                         every jade of aurora

     beating against the wind.

Reactor

Memorize the temperature
for today—the humidity, pressure
in the air, what percent chance
the skylight will turn you to soft
red, your exposed skin now a warm cartography.
Nuclear dreams do not sleep here. *Did you not hear*
  the news? This is the cure
  for loneliness. What else could it be
classified as—name, or state of mind, the heavens
grinning down on doomsday? Give your soul
to a wishing well. Write a litany
for the packrats— for every forsaken
sock left in the street, for the lost
& found, consumable darkness.
For the icemelt & acid rain.
The scarlet engine droning by itself
in the downpour. All of it is
  loveliness.

Extinction

        dusted from the universe's shoes   we were
forged by glaciers   grown in star gardens

to speak without making

a sound   astra to ascension
      words falling open   cracking

        against the hard of earth
a piece of outer space   smoldering the dinosaurs

into past lives   into names   derived from
     the human who discovered it

almost comical if it weren't so

       unnatural   or stagnant
a fly becomes trapped   & now permanent

in the amber   is doomsday
     hurdling closer   or are we

       just getting smaller?

Smash

I swear the wet of me has been wrung out
& dried by a lantern in my

      mouth igniting as I spit & split open, all flame & full

of splinters, all timber & birch,
all campfire in a cavern, all contained

      space, all tinder woven from soft wicker, all *I could burn you*

so I hope you don't mind getting a little warm because
today is Wednesday, & it's a good Wednesday

      to dance in t-shirts with the windows open

& eat scrambled eggs topped with feta cheese
while I can chant to your bristled cheek *don't say*

      it's my fault the sun finally burned me.

These wings no longer carry me
up, only down.

Emptiness Is The Mother Of All Things

Every season is rain. Every day
        falls from the clouds & dances
        down the fabric of patterned umbrellas
& I am breaking for the sake of breaking

like hazardous weather or the news
or a glow stick rattled into neon.
        we separate the body
from the body, break bread

        over blood, every week another
off-brand apocalypse weighted down
by closed-off doors & shitty megachurches
& Notre Dame scorched. We don't have time

to record every Notre dame burning
in every Paris. My wine-stained halo wanes
heavy. I try to hold a thousand sanctuaries
in the crook of my neck. If I am shattered

& marred—if I turn translucent & you suddenly
see the light fracture through me, at least
this means I fragment into stained glass
like a church window. No socket

or space can keep out the wither.
I could scream & scream & shake
        my dead follicles into ivory
sinks, watch the strands perform ballet

down the drain, a windstorm outside
ripping the holy from my mouth.

Hematite

A kidney ore. A rose made of iron.
There are endless ways to classify

Rigid distraction. The discovery of something
Complete. Envisioning a painted landscape

Of rocks. Between the distant bluffs,
A rusted barn. A trough of water. Horses tromping

Through a dead town. An arrow pointing
To the street I drove down. I took

A breath. Polished your skin & listened to birdsong. Forget
About the iron. The way you shine, the glimmering

Byproduct of something greater. My cocoon sheds itself
When I turn off the lights. Before we can make up

A reason to go rigid, your mouth burns
Volcanic. You forget how people can be

Weathered too, paved in artificial streets, one-way
Conversations I can't keep. Talk me down,

& we both jump anyways. I can't
Take it. I don't want to be sad

In a place so beautiful.

In Which I Swallow Fire

My throat is lined with gasoline. This means, my body
is rotting, crawling with flammable maggots, soon-to-be

a cadaver with necrotic tissue. I miss you. I wish
for you on every lucky penny, in all these boneyards. I weep

in these burnt-out hallways, as if slow dancing
in a flaming vacuum, my billowing dress

a bright life jacket swaying in the flash
& drowning in photos, in a dark room where shadows

play hopscotch on the walls, our breath ebbing
while you & I stand with enough room for a god

between us. Faithfully, I wait for a place of safety. I wait
for crucibles. Our underdoing was never mutual—what does

this silent language mean, are we going back to the end
together, muscles & tendons severed, tearing

out these heartstrings one by one?

You Only Love Me When I'm Burning

My portrait is no longer lovely. I cannot stop
drowning in gasoline. Give me air

to swallow & spit out. This sharp mouth,
tongue of flint, matchstick lips—one kiss,

& it all burns redblue. The withering
is setting in, a controlled burn, my throat full

of sirens. You want me to strike like lightning
to the earth—to the world that smolders.

Breathes. This is the part where I combust
& call it spontaneous. Am I doing this right?

The worst thing about being on fire is knowing
how much you love the heat, each sliver of me

kindling to ignite, stripped to igneous glass.

Reversing Gravity

If you want to be turned upside down, you will
      not speak harshly to the bank clerk

on the phone. You will not write a story
      about a man committing arson.

You will read a Richard Siken poem
      that makes you actually want to be alive

      on a planet that could explode
at any given moment. Right now,

even: forces we will never see
      could push instead of pull, you

could be watching a storm roll in
      when suddenly, you are swimming.

Just like that, you are skydiving
      in the wrong direction.

Panic infiltrates each wall
      you build yourself into

as you run a comb through your hair
before going to bed somewhere

      in the atmosphere, & I am sorry
to tell you of this strange occurrence,

          but you deserve to know.

      Eventually, you will love something
      & regret it in the same day.

iii.

You as Apocalypse

You burn the midnight oil again. Your dogs bark at the nothing outside while you pose subtly in front of the bathroom mirror. You imagine looking like Velma Dinkley, or Mia Wallace, or some other fringe-haired, feminine badass. Freights echo from miles away. This feels like a beginning—really, look at it—you got bangs today, & an epiphany, you started singing to your houseplants, scrubbed yesterday's dishes with a bright pink sponge, & then it all goes dark. Your body, a broken steam engine, scrapes against the black. You dream of endings—the final meal on vacation, or an unmarked page after an epilogue, one last swig of amber ale before the glass stands empty. You are the earth, frozen, or maybe a still frame of it—flames void of motion, hurricanes on pause, quaking tremors halted—every bird suspended into an umbrella of night.

You as Stormchaser

Do you remember when you first heard rain, or did you feel it. Your Mimi's pistachio cake. Willow trees. Church every Sunday. Youth group every Wednesday. A birdhouse for purple martins perched atop a tall, slender pole. The sound of someone cocking a bb gun. The sound of someone shooting at a flock of geese, but *not really at them, just close enough to scare them.* Was this the beginning of a downpour, or is that something you have been told. Storms breaking over our lake. Love like water skiing. A summer cold & green. Pale yellow shirts soaked in melancholy & hung out to dry in the backyard. Laughing in a red plastic chair, fingers tangled in your braid. The soft fire of a porch light. A star burning out. We spin on plastic horses in this carnival of rain. How can you say it gets better than this.

Firefly Girl

Falling from grace was the first thing
        I learned to do quietly—stumbling
like rain. We were born from the river
& don't know of an afterlife.
Maybe it means running
against the wind. Or singing
through lighthouse windows.

God is wandering
amongst the sunflowers that face the dark.
We bleed lavender water. We seek hell
in mirrors. I swear it started with a storm
warning. It started out where I left
off searching for angels
        in the fallout—when I could
write the word *celestial*
but not *somewhere.*

Centuries ago our holiness was sleeping
with daisies. This halo feels like winter.
        I folded my fears into paper cranes.
        It started with benevolence—I was there.

Daydrinking on the River Styx

Next time I die, I want to wake up in a shiny cul-de-sac
bloodied with lingonberry bushes, where I collect myself

a handful of backyard-bred cherry bombs
to grind until the pulp clots maraschino red

& vow to give the afterlife a chance
as if I am a child again, make believing a creek

is a fairytale spring where the color
of passion matches the color of

consequence, where I pretend I am
youth-riddled, removing my eyes

to save for a sunny day—that way,
I will not have to see the planet burn.

Every Day is The End of The World

You can be re-traumatized any minute. Pain gets lodged in the body unless we take up yoga or ingest plenty of omega-3 fatty acid & drink green tea & exfoliate. Don't forget to sleep a quarter of your life away. Everybody & nobody knows about unconscious memory. We build ourselves into two-story starter homes. Paint mailboxes with purple ladybugs & happy font. Basements eat phone calls before they can get to us, meaning there are likely thousands of attempted connections that shipwrecked between concrete walls & plastic laundry baskets. A signal dropped in the airspace did not suck me down with it—I am not marooned, but still study each side of this room until I have memorized it like a map, so that the room becomes permanent somewhere. The walls above this couch are coated with painted frames, I mean, just *loaded* with photos from our summer trip to Sanibel Beach a few years back. Dried lilacs pinned up with chicken wire. A print of an elephant. A metal camera to frame memories. What do we remember now, & will we be around for it matter tomorrow? After all, the earth will be incinerated before the seeds are planted, then again afterwards. Everything eventually becomes scorched in fire, or submerged in the flooding of rivers or oceans, swallowed up by the earth & spit out like an allergy, leaving the ground to swell up & die over the course of the next four million years. Like that hellish scene in Toy Story—you know the one, with Woody & Buzz, the potato heads & slinky dogs, dinosaurs, those fairy tale creatures—we all hold hands, headed to the burner, our island of misfit toys singing *ashes, ashes, all the way down.*

Relativity Theory

Everything seems miniscule if you think
about the meaning of smallness. Try to

squint hard enough & the blur turns
to gears of butterfly eggs. I'm sharing my orange

sun with you from 700 miles away. Below the bur oak
a fallen birdnest, twig-woven. What differentiates

home from tree from wicker cage. Is it holding
something born above earth, deep within

tangles of cattail fluff & sticks & spider silk
left behind. The distance between outstretched

limbs & evening dirt. I string & unstring the same
plastic pearls beside my lonely window. Grey

feathered birds come & go. Our sky turns
to umber. A monarch uncurls in the dark.

Self-Destruction & Other Disasters to Think About

the pale of Northern Michigan
deer. About wanting something
star studded & purple. About building
a rocketship—something capable
of cosmic escape. Black holes *do* happen
overnight, *& yes, I do*
think about the waitress at Addison's
restaurant & the time I went moonlighting
at a science conference, hiding in the flock
of wings. My gasoline smile. I think about
destruction taking many forms—the collapsing
of stars, a black hole born from oblivion. My body,
with its slumped posture on the closet floor. Radium
girls in cushioned graves. Nosebleeds. Hours
spent running towards tables of strangers.
I think about paradise,
or maybe walking beside it
one day in the rain, spinning
into bed next to an animal skull, about the desert
writing songs with my name. Am I the only one
who makes this shape while breaking, am I
the only bird singing
            backwards, am I
the shuddering holding me together? This
might be another fever dream, driving
through Englewood, Kansas City,
Alameda Street—until I am bounding
across I-70, both the gun & barrel
of whiskey, the creaking hinge of a ghost town
door. I think about the astronomical
tapestries in an Air BnB off Don Gaspar,

the holes in canyon walls, a case
of bullets. Astral bodies. About how
I don't know the right way
to contain this wild
energy, how I don't know who I am
working behind this hotel bar, feeding mules
to wedding guests of people I don't know
      & when I write a letter
to the universe, the only thing
that ever comes out
is another cluster
      made of stars.

From a Garden on Earth

I like to drink from the garden hose,
letting water sputter in large drips

down my chin. The birds are watching
& I cannot sing loud

enough for them to hear it:
the birds are looking

but they cannot hear me.

Across the street, a moment appears—
she had been painting a chair evergreen

& now she drinks champagne
from the bottle in a tire swing.

She is slouching & laughing
& yes, I am laughing, you can see it

in the way these clouds reflect
in puddles leftover from the rain.

Additional Acknowledgments

While I've spent countless hours, evenings, and cups of coffee putting my soul into this book, I'm especially grateful to the people who made this writing possible: my incredible family, graduate cohort at Northern Michigan University, and the English professors at both Northern and The University of Missouri who mentored me, provided endless support, and challenged my perspectives on poetry. In particular, I'd like to thank Rebecca Pelky, Bradley Harrison Smith, Gabriel Fried, and Patricia Killelea—your personal and academic encouragement has truly changed my life. A special thanks to The Sunshine Workshop for giving the feedback I needed to make these poems sing.

To Jaspal Singh, my thesis director, my mentor, and my creative inspiration: I don't know where I would be without you. Thank you for always believing in me.

Additionally, I extend gratitude to Daisy Crane for her lovely and expressive cover art, and to the writers who took the time to carefully read this manuscript and share their own words on it: Brenna Womer and Matt Mitchell. And of course, thank you to Finishing Line Press for seeing something meaningful in my work and believing in my first book. Without them, this short collection would not be in your hands right now.

And of course, none of this work would be possible without my loving and supportive partner. Brett Taylor, you are my world and more. Thank you for loving me through every disaster.

Lastly, if you're reading this, I'd like to thank you for sharing this experience on the page with me. For spending time with these words. For inspiring me to write with fierce vulnerability. For hopefully walking away with some sort of new consideration, thought, or emotion. It means everything.